MW00995589

Fantastic Fairs

Renaissance Festival

by Julie Murray

Dash!
LEVELED READERS
An Imprint of Abdo Zoom • abdobooks.com

3

Dash!
LEVELED READERS

Level 1 – Beginning
Short and simple sentences with familiar words or patterns for children who are beginning to understand how letters and sounds go together.

Level 2 – Emerging
Longer words and sentences with more complex language patterns for readers who are practicing common words and letter sounds.

Level 3 – Transitional
More developed language and vocabulary for readers who are becoming more independent.

THIS BOOK CONTAINS
RECYCLED MATERIALS

abdobooks.com

Published by Abdo Zoom, a division of ABDO, PO Box 398166, Minneapolis, Minnesota 55439.
Copyright © 2020 by Abdo Consulting Group, Inc. International copyrights reserved in all countries.
No part of this book may be reproduced in any form without written permission from the publisher.
Dash!™ is a trademark and logo of Abdo Zoom.

Printed in the United States of America, North Mankato, Minnesota.
052019
092019

Photo Credits: Alamy, iStock, Shutterstock
Production Contributors: Kenny Abdo, Jennie Forsberg, Grace Hansen, John Hansen
Design Contributors: Dorothy Toth, Neil Klinepier

Library of Congress Control Number: 2018963312

Publisher's Cataloging in Publication Data

Names: Murray, Julie, author.
Title: Renaissance festival / by Julie Murray.
Description: Minneapolis, Minnesota : Abdo Zoom, 2020 | Series: Fantastic fairs |
    Includes online resources and index.
Identifiers: ISBN 9781532127243 (lib. bdg.) | ISBN 9781532128226 (ebook) |
    ISBN 9781532128714 (Read-to-me ebook)
Subjects: LCSH: Renaissance fairs--Juvenile literature. | Ren fests--Juvenile
    literature. | Fairs--Juvenile literature.
Classification: DDC 394.6--dc23

Table of Contents

Renaissance Festival

There are more than 300 **Renaissance** festivals in the US each year. Texas hosts the biggest one. It is on 55 acres of land. More than 500,000 people attend each year!

The festival takes you back in time. Expect to see kings, queens, wizards, and fairies. The costumes worn at the festival can be **elaborate**. Many people even talk like they are from the time period.

Entertainment and Food

There is a lot to see and do at the festival. There are comedy acts and juggling shows. The Minnesota **Renaissance** Festival has more than 700 performers!

Flame throwers light up the festival. **Jousting** matches are also exciting. Members from **Hanlon-Lees Action Theater** joust at many festivals.

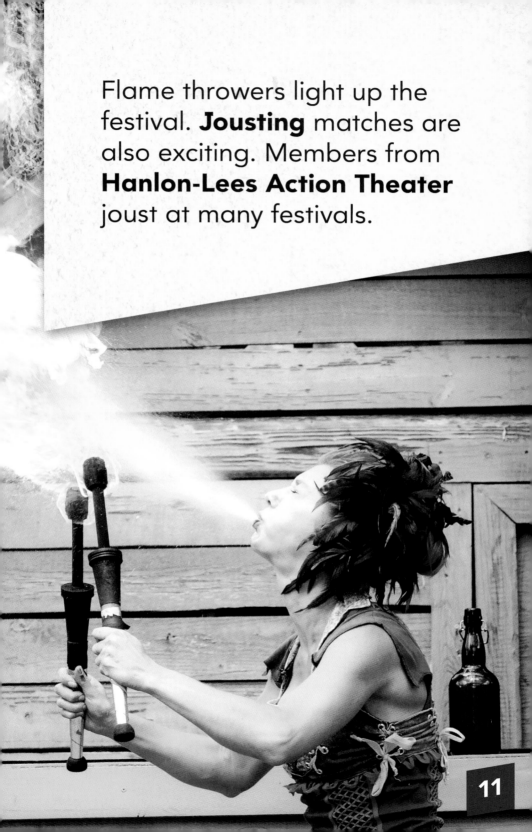

Street performers are popular. Some tell stories to crowds. There are also musical performances. Bagpipes and **crumhorns** can be heard.

You can feast like a king at the festival. Giant turkey legs and cheese fritters are popular. Some festivals serve a traditional **Renaissance** meal. It consists of soup, bread, meat, and cheese.

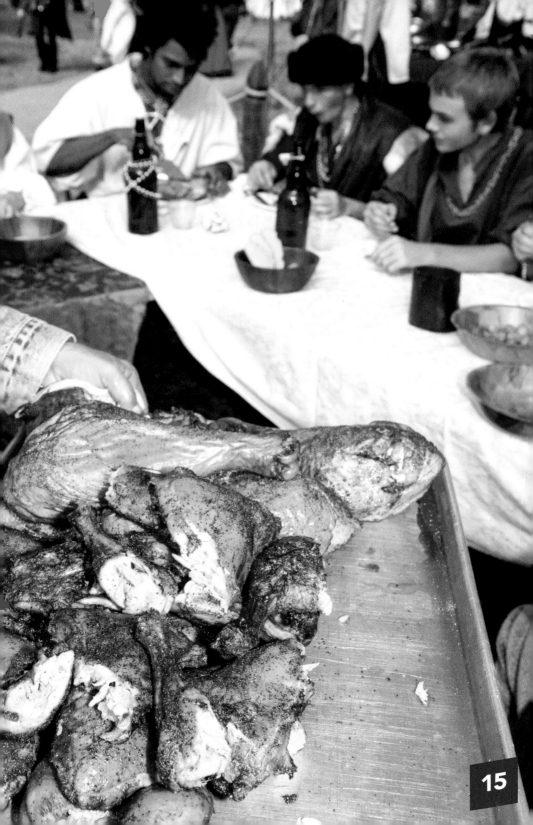

Arts and Crafts

Arts and crafts are aplenty at the festival. Potters and glass blowers give demonstrations. **Blacksmiths** also show off their talents. They make swords and knives.

There are many arts and crafts for purchase. Jewelry and wood crafts are fun finds. Many kinds of leather goods are also for sale.

The whole family can enjoy the festival. The food, costumes, entertainment, and crafts make it fun for all ages.

More Facts

- The first **Renaissance** festival was held in 1963 in California. Today, it is called the Renaissance Pleasure Faire.

- The Ohio Renaissance Festival has more than 100 shows each day on nearly a dozen stages.

- The Minnesota Renaissance Festival is one of the best in the US. It features more than 275 crafters and 120 food booths.

Glossary

blacksmith – a person who forges and shapes iron.

crumhorn – a musical instrument in the woodwind family most often used during the Renaissance period.

elaborate – very detailed in design.

Hanlon-Lees Action Theater – an entertainment company credited with the development of theatrical jousting.

jousting – a fight between two knights on horseback. Each knight tries to throw the other off his horse with a lance.

Renaissance – the revival of art, literature, and learning that began in Europe in the 1300s and lasted into the 1600s. Famous artists like Michelangelo and Leonardo da Vinci were part of it.

Index

arts 17, 18

costumes 7, 21

crafts 18, 21

entertainment 8, 11, 12, 17, 21

food 14, 21

Hanlon-Lees Action Theater 11

instruments 12

Minnesota 8

music 12

performers 8, 11, 1

Texas 5

Online Resources

Booklinks
NONFICTION NETWORK
FREE! ONLINE NONFICTION RESOURCES

To learn more about renaissance festivals, please visit **abdobooklinks.com** or scan this QR code. These links are routinely monitored and updated to provide the most current information available.